A Mexican Girl´s Long Journey

Karina Mendoza

La Pereza Ediciones

Original Title:
La larga travesía de un niña mexicana 2021
© Karina Mendoza
La Pereza Ediciones, Corp
Translated by:
Yosvani Oliva Iglesias

ISBN: 9781623751463

Design of the Collection:
Estudio Sagahón / Leonel Sagahón
and Carmina Salas
Illustrated by: Leonel Sagahón
www.sagahon.com

A Mexican Girl´s Long Journey
Karina Mendoza

LAZY

Acknowledgements

To God for giving me life and blessings
To Dr. Roger Corrales for believing in me
And to my beloved children

I always imagined that one day I could write a book. I admire a lot of Mexican writers, and that's why it seemed to me like a difficult dream to realize. I've spent a big part of my life struggling to get ahead, to survive. I am mother to three children, who are the flame that lights up my path. I want to dedicate this book to them. To them and to all the children in the world that may find themselves in extreme situations. Those children who are the future and the hope that there will come, without a doubt, better times. I also dedicate this book to my editors, Greity Gonzalez and Dago Sasiga, who, like no one, believed in my this, my humble story.

I

When one has suffered a loss or great personal pain, it becomes difficult, and I would even say it is almost impossible, to write about these events. I have suffered a lot, almost my whole life. It's taken me a long time, until now, that I'm healing emotionally, to write about my pain on these pages. My pain, which has been my life.

I thought about beginning my story by stating my name and the year I was born. Instead, I'll begin my story by introducing myself as follows.

I am a Mexican woman.

I am a Mexican woman born to the most absolute poverty.

I am a Mexican woman that migrated to the United States.

This that I am says a lot about me, right from the start.

But perhaps, what it doesn't say is that a Mexican woman like me, that was born to and grew up in poverty so common to a lost

Mexican pueblo, that overcame so many obstacles migrating to the United States, also has dreams. That she's always had them. I have not fulfilled many of my dreams, but I keep on fighting so that my children can fulfill them. And I keep fighting for myself.

When did my life really begin? I ask myself this question because there have been times when I've thought that a life does not begin when one is born. A life, I think of this often, begins with the first remembrance we have of our infancy. My earliest memory arises from a hot and dusty afternoon at the ranch where I lived with my family. That memory is a machete chopping a man to pieces. The man who wielded that machete was Sergio Mendoza, my father.

Today I'm almost convinced that my mother was responsible for so many things. What I mean to say is that any decision, as small and unimportant as it may seem, can become that which triggers everything. And I believe, and no one has ever been able to remove that idea from inside my head, that my mother's decision to not go live with my father after she became pregnant with me, was in part the cause of all her misfortunes and, of course, those of mine and my family's.

What would have happened if my mother, instead of continuing to live with my maternal grandmother, had preferred to live with my father? I have always heard that a woman ought to follow her husband, or her child's father, wherever he goes. I know that my father was only eighteen years old and my mother thirty. I know that my mother was disheartened from the failure of two prior love entanglements that only left her with children, who knows if unwanted. I know that anyone can make a mistake. Or not. Because in reality, could my mother's decision have, in the end, stop my father from hacking my uncle to death with a machete? Destiny is, whether or not it is as important as one thinks, very cruel, and not seldomly. That afternoon, at the pueblo's festival, I confirmed that to be the case.

II

December 8th, 1984 was, then, the day I was born if we take into account that one is born whenever one's first memory is. Even though I was only a year old at that time and only remember details, for the rest I was told later on. My father had become tired of waiting for my mother, and he had met another woman who, strange as it may seem it is rather common in a small pueblo, happened to his cousin's wife. And as it often happens in these seemingly strange situations, although my father and that woman kept their relationship a secret, she ended up getting pregnant by my father's cousin, or, as he was known in my family, my uncle.

It was a typical pueblo festival. All the men were drunk as usual. Everything considered, it was inevitable for my father to let his tongue loose and tell my uncle that the child his woman was carrying in her belly was his, my father's that is. They argued heatedly. But my father, I suppose with so many drinks on him, wasn't going to be content with a simple argument. He found the nearest stand where tools were sold, bought a machete, and with this weapon that, on top of it, hadn't even been sharpened, he attacked my uncle from behind. Not just once. Many times. Until dismembering him.

My father then skipped town with the woman, because, logically, my uncle's relatives wanted to kill him. Some time later, when I was four, my father went near the closest pueblo to ours to meet with my mother and gave her thirty pesos for me. They spoke for five minutes in the very early morning and then he left. I never saw him again. So, fate's ironic that way, all I was left with from that misfortune was two pants my mother bought me with those thirty pesos. And it made me so happy because I had no clothes.

What can I say about my childhood? Even people who seldon, or never at all, read the paper, know what the childhood of a poor mexican child is like. Images of children selling candy in the streets, or washing windshields at traffic lights, or simply begging anyone passing by on the street, come to mind right away. My childhood was spent at a place so, so poor, that I, even though I've never read Don Quixote, do know its first lines, and I have no shame in saying that I grew up in a place "the name of which I have no desire to call to mind." As a girl I didn't wash windshields nor sold candy, but that was simply because I did not live in Mexico City; for if not, I am certain that I would have had to do it.

But I did do similar things, the things that a mexican country child does. Night and day I prepared tortillas, tortillas that seemed infinite; I cooked beans, beans that seemed infinite, I fed every which backyard animal (not that there were many, to be sure) there was at my house; I cared for my younger brothers, the latter being something that all poor children have to do, whether they are from the country or the city; I carried heavy sacks of whatever there was on my back; I put up with the mistreatment and the bad moods of my family in full. And so on, such a long etcetera, that I truly don't think it worthwhile to continue to enumerate misfortunes.

That was my childhood.

And I'm not lacking for anecdotes.

And I won't extend on those anecdotes, although I will do it on what is known as the "the essence" of them, because that essence is my life.

III

And finally, or perhaps to begin: My name is Karina Mendoza. I was born on august the 6th, 1983, in Oaxaca State, in the pueblo of San Juan, in Juquila. There we speak a dialect known as chatino. My childhood house was a house with clay walls and a shingle roof. The utensils that we used were also made of clay. My grandmother Emilia crafted pots, plates, comales, and wooden spoons. We cooked with firewood. We dressed with huipil and nahuatl and for shoes we wore huaraches. The bed we slept in was made of a board and reed woven with twine. On top of the bed went the petate bedroll.

We're very poor. This expression, I found out many years later, is the title of short story by Juan Rulfo, a mexican writer that I first read a few years ago, and that I've found to have wonderfully dealt with the poverty of Mexico; indeed, we were so poor that my brothers and I slept embraced, so that we could all stay warm.

My family was very large, like most poor families are. It would be impossible to keep count of all my brothers, my cousins, my uncles. I mentioned before that the corn tortillas and the beans we cooked seemed endless, and this was not without reason, of course. But it also was that we never even ate any meat, nor chicken, nor fish.

There were many times when I even thought that our situation was so, simply because there were so many of us. Because my mother, my grandmother and my aunts had decided to have so many children.

I also wondered as a child what the cause for so many
births was. In what little education I received, it was always instilled in me that children are a gift from God, and I know that they are. But then I was a small girl, and I didn't understand many things. I thought that was the reason why only children that were an only child, and that we saw mainly in Mexico City, their parents holding them by the hand, could eat candy and ice cream.

I thought that was because these couples had only one child, and I thought that was the answer to everything. Just the same, and as I will tell you further ahead, I did not enforce the "one child policy" once I became an adult.

After my father murdered my uncle at the pueblo festival, which pushed him out of our lives forever, my mother found herself alone once more (if there ever was a time when she really wasn't), even while living with my grandmother Emilia and my aunt Anastasia. She got up every day before dawn, and she left to go plant corn, beans, pumpkin, anything really. Her and my aunt Anastasia, who was also a single mother to four children, left together. Sometimes my mother took me with her to the plantation, which was far from home, and I would stay there all day and night. We slept in a cave right on the hill. To me these nights are unforgettable, but not because there was something wonderful to them. To the contrary. We dressed only with leaves from plants in the forest. They were difficult days indeed. Never a lack of heat, nor rain, nor cold. We were very afraid. There were always dangerous animals on the lurk. Coyotes above all frightened us most.

But what was truly terrible for me was when my mother couldn't take me to the plantation anymore. I suppose it was because it was more comfortable to move about without a child to drag around, or heaven knows why. But she decided it was best to leave me under the care of my uncle Pánfilo and his wife Juana, who, of course, also had children.

And so it was, because of those strange things that I believe all children have, I spent all day long crying, waiting for my mom to come back, afraid that she would abandon me or that something would happen to her. I didn't eat anything, in spite of my aunt Juana's insistence. I would sit on a tree, waiting to see my mom surge on the road from one moment to another. When I would finally spother, my happiness would be so, that it made me want to eat with her, and those plates of tortillas and beans seemed to me the most delicious in the world.

When I recovered from the "trauma" of waiting for my mother every afternoon, when I eventually realized that, in the end, she would always come back, I relaxed some and began to play with my cousins Margarita, María and Brígida, uncle Pánfilo's daughters.

Happiness didn't last. Suddenly they started to hit me, without any reason, and one afternoon they had me try a mushroom that turned out to be poisonous. I almost died. My mother became so scared, watching me throw up blood and hollering from the severe stomach ache, that she sent me to another uncle's house. My uncle Eliborio Cruz. Of course, I went back to being afraid. I went back to sitting on a fence pole to wait for my mother to return from work. She then, I imagine tired from my "infantile craziness," took me back to grandma Emilia's home.

My grandmother, who before totally spoiled my aunt Anastasia's children, perhaps finally noticing everything we were going through, began to treat my brother and I a little better. Before our pilgrimage through so many uncles' houses, it was my cousins whom she would save candy for, fruits, even money and clothes. She began, as she did with pots, to craft toys from clay. Dolls, small cups, everything a toy. We, for our part, helped her clean the soil so it got thin. Because in the end, we had to contribute something to show our gratitude.

A pueblo is never short for family problems that bring with them injuries or even death. That, clearly, wasn't missing in mine, as it should be obvious by now. After being in my grandmother's house in tranquility, when we thought that everything would get better and we would be at peace, we heard a terrible shooting. At first we didn't think much of it. It was normal, after all. But then, a family acquaintance arrived and told us what happened. And everything, absolutely everything, was due to a small patch of land. A small patch of land wanted by a certain señor Carlos. And because of that small patch, he shot and wounded cousins of mine that were only children. Everything was a disaster. I really don't think it worth it to get into the details of that situation, because I can't find any meaning to it.

Everyone in my family, even I, went over like crazy innocents to see what was happening. That was our mistake. And it was a mistake because in the end we couldn't solve anything. The harm was already done. All we got was a night of sorrows and crying in the middle of the woods, running from bullets, not being able to save anyone, escaping the attention of wild animals that one of my uncles had to shoot at several times to drive them away.

Even though I have not wanted to get into details about this experience, it is fair to say that it changed our lives some. Because of fear that this señor Carlos would take it up with us, we went to live at a ranch called Pueblo Nuevo. My aunt Ernestina offered us her home. It had a palm roof and walls made of poles from the forest, a clay kitchen, and the famous beds made from sticks and twines.

Once more, I found myself surrounded by uncles and cousins, all different but the same in the end. In Pueblo Nuevo things seemed to function somewhat better, and it seemed there was a little more prosperity, but anyway it was the same. The same food. The same work rhythm. And above all, the same mentality.

Though, in regards to the mentality, I must do justice to my uncles from Pueblo Nuevo. They did want their children to go to school. The kids went to town to go to school, even though to do this they had to walk eight hours. As is only logical, they had to stay in town all week, to be able to attend school each day, and they only came back home Friday afternoon.

One of my brothers and I attended a few times, but we couldn't keep up pace. My poor mother didn't have enough money to even buy the most elementary school supplies, not to mention clothes and shoes. Anyway, I've never stopped thinking that only with a bit of extra effort from her, I could have stayed in school, but the truth is that my mother didn't give any importance to school matters. And to study is the one thing I wished for in life. I daydreamed about being able to one day become a professional. A teacher, or a doctor. Honestly, anything that would get me out of that world of poverty, ignorance and sorrows.

My sister Elizabeth was always a lot more rebellious and daring than me. She got fed up with our whole rosary of calamities and left without a doubt for the city of Oaxaca, accompanied by my cousin María. They were both eight years old. There, they sold shawls at the supply market and the stand's owner paid them with food and schooling. My sister would visit us once a year and she would stay with us for fifteen days; always bringing us small gifts that gave us a bit of happiness. Elizabeth, thanks to the not so few years she worked with that lady, was able to finish elementary school, which isn't much, but it is something, and it was, after all, a lot more than what his other brothers had.

In all her visits my sister tried to convince my mother to let her take me with her to Oaxaca, but I was still six years old and to my mother that seemed like madness. Madness eventually won, because Elizabeth never stopped talking of how wonderfully well her life in Oaxaca was going. What matters is that my mother relented and before I left she told me: "Whenever you see a red or green traffic light, it means that you are arriving in the city."

With these words, my heart started beating really fast. For the first time in my life I realized, or at the very least, I felt like never before, that I didn't know how to speak Spanish.

We arrived in Oaxaca at eight in the morning and we went to have breakfast with some friends of my sister. There, I experienced for the first time my lack of knowledge of Spanish, because I couldn't understand anything they talked about, but I didn' care. My sister didn't introduce me to her friends and I ended up standing on a corner with a plastic bag, until she arrived at one in the afternoon to get me and take me to Benito Juarez market.

We arrived at señora Silvia's stand, who sold juice. My sister ordered me to sit. I didn't know that would be the first official abandonment in my life and the beginning of many of my sorrows. After whispering mysteriously with señora Silvia, Elizabeth told me: "Wait for me, I'll be back in a few." When it became nighttime, already at nine, I knew she was not coming back.

Señora Silvia then told me: "You're going to work with me." So we left in a car and an hour later we arrived at señora Claudia's house, her neighbor. I can say that in this house I lost my childhood. I don't know how to explain it, but what I experienced there marked the end of my innocence, the innocence and happiness that no child i n the world should be without.

IV

The first night in señora Claudia's house I cried a lot, so much that I didn't managed to fall asleep til around one in the morning. Although the truth is that I had few reasons to feel nostalgic, I couldn't avoid missing my mother, my grandmother, and my whole family. The next day, at six in the morning on the dot, señora Claudia woke me up and showed me everything I had to do in the house, in exchange for only room and board. My obligations consisted of washing the taxi, sweeping the front of the house, going to get the tortillas (only then could I have breakfast), washing the dishes after lunch, and doing laundry. When washing the dishes, they had to put a shair for me at the sink because I couldn't reach. Later, logically, it was my turn to iron.

As if all of this wasn't enough, I also had to handle the shopping. When I had to go to the market, señora Claudia didn't allow me to buy meat unless it was from Doña Juanita's butcher shop, nor chicken other than from Doña Paula's chicken shop. Because of my chatino dialect everything became more difficult than it already was, and on top, the lady couldn't handle a mistake. And because I made so many of them, she scolded and humiliated me each day. She never understood that I was only a six years old girl that had to walk a lot to get to the market, and that I only dared to cross the great road that separated me from the place when another person did it. I still remember that with great sadness.

At that time, even from my limited discernment as a child, I found no improvement between the life I had led in my pueblo and this life. As a matter of fact, it seemed to me that this life was a lot worse. At least back at my pueblo I had my family, and I ate the same food I did in señora Claudia's house, and I was never humiliated. It had only been fifteen days and I already wanted to leave. Thus, señora Claudia decided to register me at the Benito Juárez school of Oaxaca; that cheered me up a little bit. I thought that so much sacrifice could be worth it if after all, I could finally go to school. I wasn't wrong, of course, but I didn't know then that in the life of a poor child, even something so simple as going to school, can also be hell.

From the beginning, everything was difficult. First, only if I finished my work at the house could I go to school, kind of like the story of Cinderella but without the dance. I always arrived late to school, and I had to get in through a hole in a broken part of the fence that I had found, since at that time the school was already closed. The teacher, as it is to be expected, scolded me. Kids would make fun of me because of the way I was dressed, with my broken huaraches and my books in a plastic bag. This situation was made worse by another development. Señora Claudia did not want me at her house any longer because I couldn't work like an adult, and the straw that broke the camel's back was the day that the teacher sent a letter to the lady, in which she stated that I was mentally retarted. She then decided to send me to señora Silvia. There, at her house, I had to work just as much or more, because not only did I bathe and fed three enormous dogs, but I also had to take out the trash each morning, when the garbage truck came by, and care for the lady's granddaughter, a baby named Abigaíl.

35

There will be no shortage of people who at this point ask themselves how is it possible that a girl born in 1983, that at the time of writing this book is only thirty seven years old, could have experienced so much hardship in a Mexico supposedly prosperous for everyone, and in the twentieth century. Well, that's how it always was and still continues to be. But not everything about my story is bad. On the contrary. I would like to make an aside to talk about a woman that changed my perception of life, of people, of the world. A teacher. My teacher Débora.

Teacher Débora was in charge of guiding the "retarded" children like me. I had ended up in this grupo thanks to the aforementioned letter sent by my previous teacher. Teacher Débora became very fond of me. I think she saw in me a girl that in reality, if I didn't learn so fast, it was because of my ingrained dialect. Thanks to the fact that she defended me since the first moment from the abusive children, and thanks to the fact that, miraculously, señora Silvia, for some strange reason unbeknownst to me, gifted me one day with a green dress that I found so beautiful, I began to believe a bit more in myself.

One day, teacher Débora invited me to go in her car to a teacher conference. I was wearing my green dress. I was in heaven. She introduced me to the other teachers and then we went to eat together at a restaurant. I was really nervous because I had never been to one, but she made me feel more comfortable when we started talking and that way I was able to enjoy one of the best chicken and rice stews I've tried in my life. I didn't know why in the middle of dinner, teacher Débora told me not to speak a word to señora Silvia about the visit to the restaurant, because, according to her, she would scold me. I didn't understand it then, but later I was able to understand it, literally, feeling the scolding burning me, even though it was another scolding, and it was on my own skin.

At señora Silvia's and her husband's house, just like at señora Claudia's house, I was never given any money, and I dreamed each night of being able to buy sweets like the other children from my school, who on occasions had gone as far as to humiliate me by throwing ice cream bars on the floor and telling me to pick them up if I wanted them; something which, of course, I never did.

One day, señora Silvia's husband left his work briefcase on the rocking chair in the living room and from there, five pesos fell on the floor and stayed laying there for days. No one noticed them. Only I would look at them. One day, I couldn't take it anymore and I grabbed the five pesos. Then I went with my brother Abel, who had also "migrated" to Oaxaca and was then working in señora Claudia's house, to buy us some sweets.

I can't remember what candy my brother got, and I bought my dream lollipop. On the way back to the house, we bumped into señora Claudia's daughter, baby Abigaíl's mother, a young woman, pretty, and very full of herself because she was in college. She didn't waste any time to go ask señora Silvia if she was giving me money.

That day I left school at six in the afternoon. When, at half past six, I opened the door to the house, all of señora Silvia's employees were there, her children, her husband, all of them there, together. They started attacking me. It seemed like a trial, except that they began to search through my bookbag, my ripped pants, through everything. Since they didn't find anything, they dragged me into the kitchen, turned the stove on and burned my hands. No one came to my help. No one believed me.

Children don't hold grudges. That's what I've heard and what I've discovered through the years. If not so, how else could it be explained that after such an experience I would continue working at señora Silvia's house? How could it be explained that I wouldn't be offended when she ordered me to pick my hair up with a ribbon when I didn't even have rubber bands, and I had to pick my hair up with strips that I ripped off from plastic shopping bags? How could it be explained that even crying, I accepted submissively that one day, for not having my hair up, she grabbed a pair of scissors and cut it like a boy, with the subsequent mockery that this later brought on me at school? How could it be explained that I got emotional because that bad woman gifted me a simple doll on Three Kings Day? How can so much abuse be explained? The answer, I believe, lies in the innocence and the sense of helplessness of childhood. And back then I wasn't even eight years old.

One Christmas day, after I was done cleaning the house, I locked myself in the bathroom, as it was my habit by then, because I didn't have any toys (two weeks later I would be gifted the doll) and I sat on the floor to count the tiles on the wall. Through the door, I heard them in the ceremony of gifts, hugs. That night I realized that I was alone in the world, but in that world I would have to fight to survive. Because of that, I began to apply myself more in school.

I began by taping up sheets of paper to the wall in front of me, when I would do laundry or wash the kitchen ware, and that way I went over the alphabet and the multiplication tables. When sweeping or cooking, I recited under my breath the lessons I had to learn. Teacher Débora was very proud of me, and when the day came to say goodbye to her, because my sister Elizabeth came for me, for me and for my brother Abel, she gave me a lot of advice that I've never forgotten.

V

We went back to el pueblo. Everyone was happy to see me. They praised señora Silvia's green dress and a pair of huaraches that she had also bothered to buy me. My cousins would touch my dress and ask me to speak Spanish to them, and for me to take them to Oaxaca so they could learn it as well.

That was a very happy day for me. I felt important, respected. But some days later something estranged happened. My mom stopped giving me attention. Now that I am an adult, I can understand that perhaps my mother was depressed.

She was still working at the plantation and I imagine that she was too tired and too worried, so as to behave with me like a normal caring mother. I'm not making excuses for her, of course, but in those days I realized that each day I would become lonelier, without anyone to go to for affection or advice.

42

One morning, I got fed up and in a rare moment of impulsiveness I decided to go back to Oaxaca. I worked in two more houses. In one of them, where I worked for six months, señor Gilberto, a violent man towards his wife, would give me five pesos each week. That's how, one peso after another, I was able to save thirtyfive pesos. I then went back to Juquila. My mother carried on with the same attitude, although my grandmother was kinder to me. My sister, always the rebel, lived night and day talking back to my mother and arguing with her over every nonsense. My mother wanted to marry her to a young man named Martín, but my sister didn't want to and after deceiving my mother, she left Juquila in the morning, walking the usual six hours. My mother was hurt by this because, for three months, we didn't know her whereabouts, nor whether she was dead or alive. One day, Elizabeth let us know through a cousin that she was fine, and with the help of Jesús, her boyfriend, whom she did fall in love with, she had set up a restaurant.

They say that all good things must come to an end and that happiness doesn't last. I think that it doesn't last long because of ignorance.

My sister paid a steep price for her ignorance. A friend of Jesús fell for her and began telling her lies about him, saying that he was cheating on her and other things of that sort. Finally, my sister believed everything she was told and like a fool ended things with poor Jesús. That's when Fernando came in, trying to win her over with roses, letters, even though in reality my sister detested him. Nonetheless, one night, she made the worst mistake possible. She got intimate with Fernando, got pregnant by him, and soured her life forever.

Of course, she got off with me, who by then was working like a beast in her restaurant. By then I felt that my life was like one of those ferris wheels at the fair, although in my case the lows outnumbered the highs. By a lot. I can say that the only happy moments in my life were those I had when I worked at señora Rosalinda's house. Señora Rosalinda and her husband were owners of a movie theater and other important businesses. Once their businesses went under because of poor decisions, and once I realized that there was no way I was going back to work in a house where I would be treated literally like a slave, I decided that the time had come for me to escape from Mexico.

VI

From the moment Rosalinda and I met, I felt like I had met an angel. I remember that the first thing she did was give me tickets to go to their movie theater, the Sala Versalles. She always helped me serve the food, and didn't let me eat in the kitchen. She always had me sit at the table with her family. I had my own room and my own bathroom. She wouldn't stop giving me gifts. I'll never forget that the Christmas I was in her house she gifted me a Barbie, the second doll I had. Rosalinda's family is what can be referred to as a well structured family, nothing dysfunctional about it. She would always take me with them when they visited relatives and even though I always enjoyed myself, I couldn't help but notice my own lack because of never having a family like hers.

I also remember that when my birthday came around, she organized a small celebration. It was the first time I had a birthday party, and still being a girl, it made me cry full of emotion.

Rosalinda would drive me to school in her car, and even though I worked hard in her house, I never felt exploited. That woman filled with love the void left by my real mother. Even though she didn't work and spent most of her time in get-togethers and going out with friends, she never turned her nose up at anyone. That is to say, she was not one of those, all too common, stuck up ladies that treat those without money as if they were inferior beings. She was a humble lady who understood that, even with all they had, they were no millionaires. Nonetheless, in the other houses I worked at, even when they had a smaller economy than Rosalinda's house, they acted as if they were wealthy. Thi is still something very common in Mexico, I think.

With time, I wanted to be as entrepreneurial as Rosalinda's family. To me, that seemed to be the solution to the life I had always had. That's how,with the money Rosalinda paid me, I was able to save up a decent amount to start my own business selling food. She gave me a few wares and a blender. As it is to be expected, since I had no support from my family, the business failed and my happiness, once more, didn't last long.

One day, my paternal grandfather, Ginio Mendoza, came into my life. He was by then eighty five years old with a forty years old wife. He wanted to take me to live with him in an enormous house he had, since he had managed to cultivate some lands that produced a great amount of coffee. Of course, his wife immediately had it out for me in fear that I would claim part of my grandfather's inheritance. I decided that I had already lived through enough humiliations, so one afternoon I went with my grandfather to a supply store, and since I didn't have the courage to tell him I was leaving, I asked him, without lying, to wait for me, that I had to go to my school for some papers. I, indeed, picked up the papers, and once more I went to Rosalinda's house. If it were up to me I would have spent my entire life working at that house, but faith can be cruel and it had very different plans, not only for Rosalinda and her family, but also for me.

I had previously mentioned that Rosalinda's family had fallen in financial ruin. Her father in law began having problems, and with him, the rest of them. They had to take all of their children out of private school and Rosalinda herself, who had never worked, started giving English lessons to assist financially in the house. It pained me to see her suffer, and it pained me more having to leave because they couldn't afford to pay me anymore.

Thereby, I had to go back to looking for houses where to work. I went through three more, and even though by then I was getting paid, I was fed up with being a servant. School became ever more expensive, and because of it I could only go as far as my second year of middle school. At that time, I began to feel like my life had reached its end. Was that all there was for me to do? Work eternally? In those days there were times I had two jobs, one of them at a hotel. I was exhausted, more mentally than physically.

The way things were, my family's insistence that I left for the United States became inevitable. My mother wanted to send me to Atlanta, Georgia, where my brother in law Fernando lived. I really didn't want to go. Not only was I afraid, I also didn't have the money to pay a coyote: twenty thousand pesos was the going rate, an amount that I hadn't seen in my life. But I was so overwhelmed that I relented and asked one of my cousins for help. She lent me ten thousand pesos at ten percent interest. Another lady, named Regina, lent me the other ten thousand at the same rate.

I must say this. I felt like a useless object that everyone just wanted to be rid of. But I didn't blame anyone, even though I knew no one would miss me even if I died. While going through all this, I would often wonder, what have I been good for? To clean other people's houses? I know that it was honest work. Working in someone else's house is no less honest than sweeping streets or picking up garbage. Nonetheless, that's how I felt in those days, that my family wouldn't bat an eyelid if I left. I was already eighteen years old, and since the age of six all I had ever done was clean houses, with greater or lesser luck. To make matters worse, they all wanted, in the end, to be rid of me. Even I felt like it was my fault. I felt that I was devoid of character. Perhaps, had I faced my grandfather's wife, my fortune would be different, and I wouldn't find myself, as I was about to be, crossing a desert that I had never even seen.

Every time that I said goodbye to a member of my family, I felt a part of me dying. It was emotional death; the type you know that you can't turn back from in a thousand years. Not even if you become a millionaire in your dream land. A strange death that keeps you from happiness even if you find everything you once dreamed of. Because, for better or worse, that was my family. My mother, my grandmother, my siblings, my poor patch of land. But the worst part, the saddest part, was saying goodbye to grandma Emilia, who was ninety years old, but who nonetheless accompanied me to the taxi station with her inseparable cane, and gave me her blessing.

VII

Who am I to talk about the journey of a Mexican woman through the desert? I am nobody. Others, real writers, have narrated it with a mastery that I could never achieve. Not to mention film directors that have made such great movies. But as you surely know, no fiction can surpass reality.

What I describe here can't come close to what I really experienced, what I and my companions really felt in those days of horror and uncertainty. A man from Veracruz helped some of us, who didn't know how to swim, to get across the Rio Grande. Once we reached the other side, that is to say, once we were in the United States, we were barely given a minute to get dressed, and then we ran like maniacs from the migra trucks that were chasing us. Luckily, they were far enough that it gave us enough time to get away. Somehow, we had to get to the road where the coyote was waiting for us. Once there, we were piled up in three trucks. I found myself crushed between four people the entire trip. The driver kept telling us in every imaginable expletive not to move, even if we couldn't breathe, because it could cause the truck to move, attracting the police. We spent half an hour in that wretched truck until we reached Brownsville county, in Texas. There, we stayed in an abandoned house, from where we could hear the sound of the immigration helicopter. After four days, when everything was calmer, the coyote gave each of us a bag with canned food and two gallons of water, and took us to another road through which we would go by every immigration check-point. We had to reach San Antonio, Texas.

We only walked at night. We were in the desert for three days. The first night we went to sleep very tired and we hid between dried trees. I can't forget a young lady, Rosy, that couldn't endure the walk because she was wearing a new pair of shoes that fit tight. She had horrible blisters in her feet. Two men carried her for a while. She would cry and say that she couldn't take the pain anymore, imploring to just be left there. It made me wonder how is it possible for someone to let oneself die so easily. That's how much pain that poor girl was in. My guess is that she couldn't find a better pair of shoes, but it could be even worse: to have to walk barefooted across that desert. The coyote decided that it was best to drug her so she could get through it; but when the drug's effect wore off, the pain returned and she went back to hollering, and then more drugs. It was hell.

On the first day, we saw a mother with her baby. They were both dead. You could tell, in horror, that they had been dead for several days. The mother was in such a position that it was easy to see that she had tried to protect her daughter from the burning sun, in the shade of a cactus. That was the picture.

When I saw that, when I saw that none of us could do anything for that woman and her baby, I asked myself, for the first time in my life, why; I mean to say, why was this the life that we were given? Why did it have to be mexicans, central americans, the poor folk of the world, who had to go through this? Was it our government's fault? Was it the United States government's fault? Was it our fault? I even asked myself whether it was God's fault.

But there was no time for sorrow, even if it were in your soul. On the second day, a man laid down on a large rattle snake's nest. We were all so frightened we didn't dare say a word. The man, bit by bit, slowly crawled away from the snake. One of our travel partners grabbed a stick and was able to kill it. Once dead, we all saw it there, thick, long, of about three meters. I thought that, in a way, even that animal was a victim of our fate.

That morning, after the experience with the snake, we kept walking all afternoon and all night, exhausted from carrying the food and water. Since we couldn't throw that away, I left a thick sweater and a pair of pants in the desert. Others did the same.

A Salvadoran man had the audacity to curse back at the coyote and he, of course, put a gun to his head. Very little after the Salvadoran man got on his knees pleading for his life, and the coyote forgiving him, and me thinking at that moment that maybe the coyote could also be Salvadoran, we arrived, after other similar and no less terrible drawbacks, to real American soil.

Just like some of my travel partners, the first thing I did when we stopped at a gas station was to buy the smallest hamburger I could find with the little money I had. And after another four hours on a new trip, this time inside the promised land, I arrived in Atlanta, where my brother in law Fernando was waiting for me. We had dinner at a Mexican restaurant and the next day we went to an employment agency, where I immediately found work at a restaurant in Harrisburg, Virginia. As it was to be expecte d, no one spoke Spanish. The story of my life was repeating itself, this time with English. Once again I was missing my family, and even Rosalinda, whom I dreamt of each night. Logically, I was fired just a few days later for not knowing how to speak English. They put me on a Greyhound bus and sent me back to Atlanta. As it was, I understood, or at least I thought I did, that had I been the owner of that business, I would have done the same thing.

By the time I arrived in Atlanta, I had prepared myself for the worst. On the bus, I met another Salvadoran man (every time I looked at him, and I couldn't help but look, it seemed to me that I was again seeing the rattle snake from the desert) who sat next to me. I told him what I was going through and he said he would help me. Now I realized that I was being reckless, but then… How was I supposed to know that in the United States not speaking to a stranger is basic knowledge? I was fortunate. This gentleman helped me find work at a plastic and juice factory, right along another job I found at a McDonald's branch. I never stopped working. I had to pay my debt with the coyote. At McDonald's I met Yadira, with whom I started a great friendship. She was a single mother to two sons and she offered me to go live with her and share expenses. After three months, they started asking for legal papers at the factory and since I didn't have them, I was let go. I was full of shame in front of Yadira. Now I only had the McDonald's job, and my debt in Mexico was skyrocketing. But I was lucky, if you can call it luck, to find another job at a restaurant as a dishwasher. At least there was a countryman I could speak Spanish with. His name was Filemón. We could speak Spanish and help each other. That's how I was able to hold the job for six months, until, finally! I was able to pay my debt with the coyote.

One day I decided, because after all, or because of it all, I couldn't be nor act any other way, to save up to build my mother a decent house. A Chinese cook, seeing that I worked so hard, gave me a card for an agency in New York where he assured me I would find a better job. I wasn't too keen on it, and something happened that one thinks only happens in soap operas. While I was talking to the cook, I noticed that Filemón was listening in on us. His father was unemployed in North Carolina. It didn't take a rocket scientist to realize that if Filemón had his ear stuck to the other side of the door, it was because he was already thinking of a way to get me fired from the restaurant and get his father the job.

Frightened, but convinced that it was better, before I was let go, to leave of my own accord, I set out on the long trip to New York, to, like a maniac, search for the agency that the aforementioned Chinese cook had told me about.

And that's how, suddenly, I arrived in Pennsylvania. To me, it was the same as arriving in the middle of Manhattan. At this point I should perhaps say that I think I've been, in spite of the misfortunes brought on by the fatality of being born where I was, a lucky woman. After just a few days, I began working at a restaurant. King of Prusia was its name. Because the world is such a small place, at this restaurant, a man called Pedro, who was from Puebla, also worked as a cook, and he helped me a lot with my English. I was being paid fourteen hundred dollars a month and I was as happy as a clam. I talked on the phone with my cousin Elvia and my brother Abel. They had also gone through the well-known journey and now resided in Orlando. And I say resided, because saying that they lived would be an exaggeration for a person without papers, in a country where, without warning, your life may change in a minute. Since my brother also wanted to come to New York, I found myself another job as a busgirl, so that my brother could take the job as dishwasher helper. In the end, the three of us decided to go for it in New York. Seeing so many buildings, so many faces out on the streets, it was like a dream to me. I even felt like a rich woman! We went up the Empire State building, which I know many people are afraid to go that high, but once you've gone through the desert you don't fear anything. Once, we even saw Madonna and Britney Spears from a distance. We felt, naively, that anything was possible in New York; but we weren't able to find work and we decided to return to Pennsylvania. We each started working at different factories. After six months, my brother left for Iowa. He had met a girl from there. For my part, the factory I was working at went under and we were all let go.

It has taken me a lot of effort, of every kind, to assume a calm attitude as an immigrant. Because for an immigrant in the United States -I know it is very similar, maybe even worse, in other parts of the world- living undocumented is to live in anxiety and worse, it is to live in an eternal shadow. But I think I've managed it.

I moved back to Orlando with my cousin Elvia, to live in a mobile home with more people; more than there should have been. It was a horrible mess.

So it was a blessing, beyond the economic matter, to find work in a hotel cleaning bathrooms. There's no need to say that it was hard work and poorly compensated. Anyone knows that or can at least imagine it, but I had no other option. Besides, it was a relief to get away for a few hours from the madness at the house in which we lived.

And that way, while I cleaned toilets in the hotel, I even got to think of myself as a blessed woman, because it distracted me from thinking much about the disaster that happened with the construction of my mother's house. Since I didn't trust her nor my sister Elizabeth, I would send the money for the works to my cousin Flor, who would tell me that it was all worthless because everyone was always fighting over the money. Because, after all, no one cared about building a decent house; only about spending the money on anything. The house was never finished, and I felt stupid. There's no need to mince words.

VIII

One day, there arrived a man at my workplace who, at least in my eyes, was the most handsome one I had ever seen. His name was José Gabino and once he saw me, the first thing he did was come near me and offer to help with my work. Because I said no, he got upset and didn't talk to me for many days. At the time, I didn't understand his reaction. How could I tell him that it was embarrassing to let him help me to finish cleaning a bathroom? Since I was a small child I was told that cleaning a bathroom, along with many other household chores, wasn't the work of men. Later, I learned that José was one of those men who don't take no for an answer. Even if it was the silliest no in the world. As it was, with time I started going out with him. I was deeply in love. I think he was too. We walked as much as forty minutes to see each other, because neither of us had a car. As it often happens when two people love each other and are poor, and don't have a lot of options (not to go out to nice places, nor travel, or they simply don't have the education that would allow them to spend time just talking about interesting things), the inevitable happened: I got pregnant. And with that naivety that is common among poor folk, we both were happy. We didn't think about the real consequences and the responsibility that it is to bring a child into the world. Both of us were so young, with no money, with nothing.

When you don't have anything, you tell yourself, and you keep repeating it, that you have nothing to lose. And so little to lose we had, that with nothing but our innocent happiness, we moved into another mobile home. The people who lived there drank a lot. Of course, José wasn't going to be outdone. He was a man. I was just the pregnant woman that on the next day had to pick up the empty cans of cheap beer and clean up the mess.

With my submissive attitude, I think that, maybe with another woman things would have been different, it was inevitable for the day to come in which José, due to the drinking, would get violent and attack me. It was only a push. Certainly. But now that I've learned more about life, I've read that abuse is abuse and that it is not only physical, but emotional as well. I was hurt by that blow, but above all, I felt humiliated.

The next day José asked for my forgiveness, with the classic oath that it wouldn't happen again and that we would soon leave that place. I didn't want to forgive him. Now, writing these lines, I would like to explain my decision. How could I, who, since I was a small child, had been so mistreated, who had, in all, such a sad childhood, play hard to get with José's pleading? No one had ever pleaded with me. No one had ever promised me anything. That's why I forgave him.

One day Pablo, José's brother, arrived at our house and we went back to the spiral of violence. Pablo would incite José to go out in my car everyday, while I had to walk long distances to buy diapers for our child. They drank at all times and, to make matters worse, because of the chauvinist ideas Pablo would put in his brother's head, I had to give José my entire pay.

One day, tired of it, I argued with my husband. That day I received my second beating. Fearing for my life and because this time it wasn't only about me, there was also my son, I escaped how I best was able to and I called the police. They detained José and he was arrested for twenty days. As is often the case in these situations, love got the better of me and I dropped some of the charges that I had filed against him, and he went free with a year on probation.

By then, even though we continued to live together, I already wanted to separate from him. I wasn't happy. I asked my mom for advice in a phone call, and she got offended and argued that none of my cousins had ever abandoned their husbands. I didn't bother to question that nonsense, and I call it nonsense because, after all, my mom was never a role model worth following. So I promised myself not to consult anything else with her nor with anyone else in my family. I comprehended then, that all of them acted in the shadow of an ignorance that did not allow them to see beyond the only horizon that they had the rotten fortune to see.

After eight months of pregnancy, in which I didn't stop working a single day, on top of it putting up Jose's constant aggression, Kelly Michelle was born. Ì had conflicting feelings. I felt happy and sad at the same time, because I could only see a baby that was coming into the world to suffer her father's mistreatment, and who knows how many other men's.

We had to leave from the house we were living in, because one night, in one of the many benders there were, the men started arguing, breaking ornaments, throwing bottles, destroying everything. A neighbor called 911 and in a whiff, the house was surrounded by patrol cars and helicopters flying over our heads. They made all of us come out with our hands above our heads, pointing at us with their weapons. I don't think I had ever felt so much fear, not even in the desert. I saw myself dying in that instant and I could only think about my children. That made me want to fight even more, if that's possible, for them, for their future. I didn't want this life for these poor angels.

Around that time, I began working at a Marriott hotel. I was doing pretty well except for the continuing issues with my husband, until one day that he got home, packed up some clothes and let me know that we were getting separated. Soon, I found out he was involved with some woman named Eliza, who also worked at the hotel. At first I didn't want to believe it, but eventually I had to face reality. And so are the whims of a woman scorned, at that moment I felt that I loved him again. But he, surely knowing that he had the advantage, humiliated me; he wouldn't let me touch him; he wouldn't eat what I cooked for him; he would constantly tell me that I was ugly. He would even scream out loud in front of my co-workers that he would marry Eliza at the first opportunity. My self esteem dropped to the floor and I felt that things needed to change and that only I could change them. So the first thing I decided to do was to leave that hotel and, thanks to a friend, I found work at a Hard Rock Café. I also started getting counseling from a psychologist, who recommended that I started group therapy, from where I came out much more strengthened.

Later on, because apparently my life, still a young one, has been that of a globetrotter, I was fired from my job. I found another one in Tampa. The pay was terrible and I even had the electricity cut off. With help from the psychologist, I was put in a mobile home with two months of rent paid and everything included. Around that time, José found Eliza with another man and that's how, after thinking it over, I got back with him. I thought I had to do it for my children, so they could have a father around. The father I didn't have.

Then my youngest was born, Kevin Alexander. By then, I was tired of working so much and I desired to go back to Mexico. I missed my family. And so one day, without giving it much thought, José and I left. We took advantage of the fact that we got money returned in our taxes going back three years and we set off on our journey back to our land. Once we arrived, right away we started spending money on food, hotels and legal procedures for a truck whose papers we wanted to put in legal order. After a thousand obstacles, we arrived at José's pueblo, Franco Madero, in Chiapas. My eyes encountered a desolate landscape. It was something I didn't remember, or that I didn't want to remember: the dirt roads, the dust and, most horrible, those faces where one could see so much poverty that it hurt.

José's family was also poor, but they didn't lack haughtiness. When we arrived at the house, we were received with joy and it became patently manifested when we opened up the gifts. Only that, once the gifts and the money ran out, so did the happiness. It didn't surprise me. Besides, what I wanted most was to visit my mom and my grandmother Emilia. It had been more than ten years without seeing them. My mother in law, with the regional prejudices so typical of the pueblos, especially the more backward pueblos, opposed that José and I went alone, with the peculiar argument that everyone from Oaxaca was a bad person. I deduced from her reasoning that she also considered me a bad person. In total, six people went along with us, and surely, they were marveled with the beauty of my birthplace's beaches and its effervescent tourism. Undoubtedly, the place looked very different, but it still maintained that sad air from souls that get old without seeing much beyond themselves.

The first thing I did was visit my grandfather Ginio Mendoza. At first, he didn't want to open the door because the day before he had been assaulted, but once he opened we had a wonderful night, full of conversations filled with nostalgia. The next morning we fried fish and drank coffee. To me, everything had the taste of my land, which I had almost forgotten and everything seemed wonderful to me.

That wonder ended once, full of nerves, something I consider incomprehensible when visiting a mother happened. I arrived at her house and hugged her. My nerves weren't unfounded. After the brief and dry hug, she became indifferent about my arrival and told me that I didn't matter to her anymore, that the only thing that mattered to her were my brothers. I didn't reply to her. I left to go see my grandmother, by then a 104 years old elderly lady. She recognized me right away and took my hand saying that she was happy to see me before dying.

Once back in José's house, the problems began: this time of a different kind. Even though throughout the length of my marriage to him I never stopped helping his family economically, it seemed as if they lived only to bad mouth me. And José never took my side. I decided to buy some land and I made plenty of money out of it. Deep inside, I thought naively, that perhaps, why not? I could become rich in Mexico. But in the end, it was nothing but obstacles and envy from my husband's family. All this considered, and also that my son Kevin Alexander became ill during the trip, with the consequent exorbitant expenses of his treatments, drove me to make the decision to go back to the United States, from where perhaps we shouldn't have left. In fact, if it weren't because I was able to see my grandfather Ginio and my grandmother Emilia, in retrospect, that trip didn't make any sense.

We decided that José would leave first and I would follow. Because we didn't have any money, we asked for a loan and, thanks to the endorsement from a friend and the truck's title, we got it. When José left, a calvary ensued with the coyotes, who never stopped asking me for more money than agreed upon. Money that I didn't have. I sold three cows, I borrowed, I did anything, and nothing was enough. Finally, after many misfortunes and much pleading, they set José free in Orlando and I readied to leave, with my soul in pain, for, to make matters worse, I had to leave my children behind with my husband's family.

IX

So I repeated the nightmare of crossing the desert once more, and it was a much more terrible nightmare than the first one, because I couldn't stop thinking of my children. When I arrived in Orlando, José and I worked hard to send to Mexico everything they needed. But I cried every night because, after all, I couldn't give them what is most important: a kiss, my motherly warmth, my love. In my desperation, I remembered Rosalinda, who could travel legally to the United States. I asked her, out of charity, to bring my little children. She asked me for some time to bring it up with her husband. José and I wrote a letter authorizing Rosalinda to travel with my children. The day I saw them arriving at the airport, I cried out of joy. I cried out of love. I think it was the happiest day of my life. I'll never be able to repay Rosalinda for everything she's done for me.

One day, through the window, I saw José doing drugs with a friend. I was so disappointed by it, after everything that we had been through together, that I fell into another depression and this time, I felt I was never going to come out of it. That action by José made everything make sense: his bad moods, his outbursts, his lack of money, his thinness. The children were also afraid of him; it wasn't only me.

One night, one of many in which I couldn't sleep thinking that something bad may happen to him, José, who was driving drunk, hit the sign of an auto repair shop. The owner wanted to call the police, so we had to pay a good amount of money to fix that disaster. Because of that, we had to eat salted tortillas for two months. My children could eat at school, but I was desperate. I couldn't avoid thinking of my childhood and I could only think of how I had spent my life going around in circles.

After that event, José tried to change and he was almost another man when, one day, when going to work, he was stopped by immigration agents, and, since he had had many charges since 2008, he was arrested and this time there was nothing that could be done.

Once more, I was alone. Alone and with my children, fighting for them. Alone. As it has always been in my life.

My humble story is yet to have an ending. Neither a sad one nor a happy one. My journey continues, and I know that I still have to walk through a long road ahead of me, before I can find at least the tranquility I so desire for me and for my family, and especially for my children. I have the good fortune that they are noble children and very smart.

I want for them everything I didn't have, especially an education. Right at this moment, I am aware that had I had the possibility to study when I arrived in this country, my life would be very different today. But I couldn't. Not can I now. As an undocumented woman, I am invisible in this land. And I don't want this future for my children, because if it were to be that way, none of what I've sacrificed would have been worth it.

Just recently, José Abisai, my oldest, has taught me how to use a computer, and through it I've discovered a world I didn't know existed, and I feel that maybe it's possible, that perhaps I can start studying with the same energy I washed dishes with for a minimum wage. On top of that, when José Abisai tells me that he wants to be a doctor and I see that Kevin

Alexander has great talent for drawing, I think everything is a matter of mindset, that it does not matter if you grow up in poverty and in a marginal environment. What's important is that you overcome those deficiencies and that you open your mind to the fact that there's a place out there, far from the scarce resources where you've lived, and that there is knowledge in that place, culture, intelligence, common sense. And that place is where you can find the beauty of life.

My story can be the story of millions of women, and not only Mexican women, but also from other Latinamerican countries. It is not a simple thing to be born poor and to grow up in a hostile environment, full of prejudices. Not is it easy to emigrate alone to a country not knowing the language, nor a thousand other things that one has to know before entering "the promised land." More still when you emigrated practically forced by circumstances imposed on you by others. Regardless, I hold no grudges towards anyone. Not even towards my husband. As a matter of fact, I call him on the phone whenever I can and I try to encourage him. I ask him to keep the faith, the sun always rises, for as long as we have health, hope and a God above, dawn will always come.

I, Karina Mendoza, am a survivor from almost everything in the world, but I am, firstly, a woman that believes in hereams and tries to reach them. And a woman who if she doesn't get there at first, anyhow, she will keep on trying, for her and her children. That's why I said that my journey continues, and it will be a long one, to my good fortune. And that's why I state here that this book doesn't end here, in this last page, but that in reality, it is only the beginning of everything that is to come, and because of the experiences I've lived, I know there will be a lot of good and of happiness.

9 781623 751463